What Do You Find in a Coral Reef?

Megan Kopp

Crabtree Publishing Company

www.crabtreebooks.com

Author
Megan Kopp

Publishing plan research and development
Reagan Miller

Editors
Janine Deschenes
Crystal Sikkens

Design
Ken Wright
Tammy McGarr (cover)

Photo research
Janine Deschenes
Crystal Sikkens

Production coordinator and prepress technician
Ken Wright

Print coordinator
Katherine Berti

Illustrations
Barbara Bedell: page 21 (coral with fish)
Katherine Berti: page 21 (sun on coral)
Margaret Amy Salter: page 21 (sea turtle background)
Tiffany Wybouw: page 21 (sea turtle)

Photographs
Thinkstock: pages 7, 8
All other images from Shutterstock

Library and Archives Canada Cataloguing in Publication

Kopp, Megan, author
    What do you find in a coral reef? / Megan Kopp.

(Ecosystems close-up)
Includes index.
Issued in print and electronic formats.
ISBN 978-0-7787-2257-1 (bound).--ISBN 978-0-7787-2277-9 (paperback).--
ISBN 978-1-4271-1723-6 (html)

    1. Coral reef animals--Juvenile literature. 2. Coral reef biology--
Juvenile literature. 3. Coral reef ecology--Juvenile literature. I. Title.

QH541.5.C7K67 2016   j591.77'89   C2015-907988-8
                                                C2015-907989-6

Library of Congress Cataloging-in-Publication Data

Names: Kopp, Megan, author.
Title: What do you find in a coral reef? / Megan Kopp.
Description: New York, New York : Crabtree Publishing Company, [2016] |
    Series: Ecosystems close-up | Includes index.
Identifiers: LCCN 2015047294 (print) | LCCN 2015047592 (ebook) | ISBN
    9780778722571 (reinforced library binding) | ISBN 9780778722779 (pbk.)
    | ISBN 9781427117236 (electronic HTML)
Subjects: LCSH: Coral reef animals--Juvenile literature. | Coral reef
    ecology--Juvenile literature.
Classification: LCC QL125 .K67 2016 (print) | LCC QL125 (ebook) | DDC
    578.77/89--dc23
LC record available at http://lccn.loc.gov/2015047294

Crabtree Publishing Company

Printed in Canada/032016/EF20160210

Published in Canada
Crabtree Publishing
616 Welland Ave.
St. Catharines, Ontario
L2M 5V6

Published in the United States
Crabtree Publishing
PMB 59051
350 Fifth Avenue, 59th Floor
New York, New York 10118

Published in the United Kingdom
Crabtree Publishing
Maritime House
Basin Road North, Hove
BN41 1WR

Published in Australia
Crabtree Publishing
3 Charles Street
Coburg North
VIC 3058

Contents

What is a Coral Reef?

Coral is a living animal. All coral animals have soft bodies. There are two types of coral. One type of coral grows a hard shell over its body. The other type of coral does not.

Sea fans are a type of coral that does not grow a hard shell. They are soft coral that move and bend with the water.

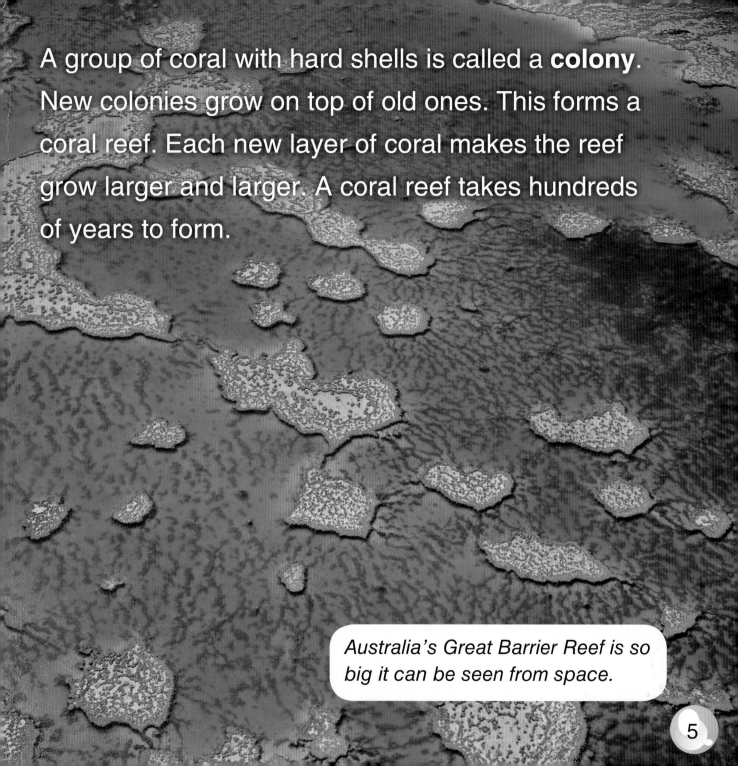

A group of coral with hard shells is called a **colony**. New colonies grow on top of old ones. This forms a coral reef. Each new layer of coral makes the reef grow larger and larger. A coral reef takes hundreds of years to form.

Australia's Great Barrier Reef is so big it can be seen from space.

The Coral Reef Ecosystem

Systems are made up of connected parts. If one part is missing, it does not work well or at all. An **ecosystem** is a type of system made up of all the living and nonliving things found in one place.

The living and nonliving things in a coral reef ecosystem are all connected.

An Underwater System

A coral reef is an underwater ecosystem. It includes living things such as plants and animals. Living things grow and change. Plants make new plants. Animals have babies. Nonliving things are not alive. They do not change or grow. Water, rocks, and sunlight are some of the nonliving things found in a coral reef ecosystem.

Fish, plants, and coral itself are some of the living things found in a coral reef ecosystem.

Life on a Coral Reef

Plants and animals need both nonliving and living things in order to survive, or stay alive. Plants need sunlight, air, and water to grow. Animals need water, air, food, and **shelter** to survive. Plants and animals can only live in an ecosystem that gives them everything they need.

Adult sea turtles depend on coral reef plants for food to survive.

Working Together

All of the living and nonliving things in a coral reef ecosystem work together. **Algae** use sunlight to grow on the coral reef. Sea urchins eat the algae. By eating the algae, the sea urchins clean the coral and keep the algae from overtaking the reef. This allows other animals to use the reef for food and shelter.

1

Algae grow in sunlight

2

Urchins eat algae

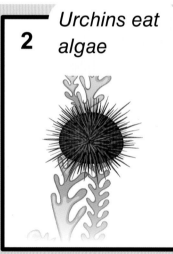

3

Fish feed on clean coral reef

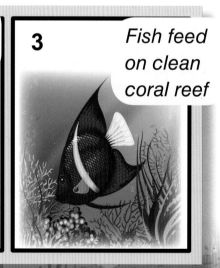

*Scientists use **models** such as this coral reef storyboard to help us understand how systems work together.*

Breathing Underwater

All living things need air to live. Air is a nonliving thing. Most of the animals found on coral reefs spend their whole lives underwater. They need to get their air from the water.

Air is found all around the coral reef ecosystem.

Taking in Air

Shrimp, crabs, and fish have special body parts called **gills**. Gills allow them to breathe under the water. Large animals, such as sea turtles, have lungs. They cannot take air out of the water. They need to come to the surface to breathe.

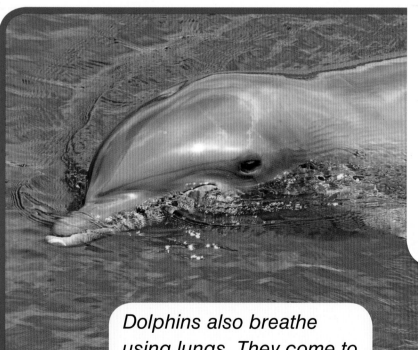

Dolphins also breathe using lungs. They come to the surface to take in air.

What do you think?

Using information on this page, explain how living and nonliving things are connected in a coral reef ecosystem.

So Much Water, Everywhere!

All living things need fresh water to survive. Fresh water does not have salt in it. Coral reefs grow in oceans that contain salt water. The plants and animals living in a coral reef ecosystem have ways of taking in the salt water and getting rid of the salt in it. They are then able to use the water.

Fish often get rid of extra salt when they urinate, or pee.

Taking it in

Many coral reef animals drink the salt water. Some animals, such as sharks and fish, take in water through their gills. Other reef creatures get water from the foods they eat.

What do you think?

Besides taking in water, what else do animals such as fish use gills for?

Sea turtles drink salt water. They get rid of extra salt using special "salt **glands**" behind their eyes.

A Seafood Diet

All living things need food to live and grow. Food gives living things **energy**. Plants make their own food using sunlight, air, and water. Plants only grow on shallow reefs where sunlight can reach.

There is plenty of sunlight shining on this coral reef near Africa.

What do you think?

Look at the next page. What might happen to the eel if seagrass was not able to grow on a coral reef?

Time to Eat!

Animals can't make their own food. Some animals eat plants for energy. Butterflyfish nibble on seagrass. Some animals eat other animals. Eels eat small fish such as the butterflyfish. The movement of energy from one living thing to another in an ecosystem is called a **food chain**.

butterflyfish

sea grass

eel

This image shows the flow of energy through a food chain in a coral reef ecosystem.

Home Sweet Coral Reef

One out of four animals found in the ocean live on a coral reef. Coral reefs provide shelter for many animals. Shelter is a place where animals can hide and stay safe from other animals that might want to eat them. It is also a safe place to have babies.

Coral reef sponges provide shelter for fish and shrimp.

A Safety Net

The sea anemone is an animal that stays in one place on a coral reef. It protects clownfish and their eggs by giving them shelter. In return, clownfish eat the small animals that might hurt the sea anemone.

Crabs hide from other animals in cracks, or between coral branches.

Sea anemone and clownfish

Protecting Coral Reefs

Coral reefs are beautiful places to explore, but they are in trouble. Coral reefs are sensitive to change. Development along coastlines causes soil to wash into the water. This makes the water dirty, and blocks sunlight. Without sunlight, plants cannot grow.

Seas are also getting warmer. This change is causing coral reefs to die like this one. Living things that depend on the coral reef can no longer survive here.

What can we do?

When we visit a reef, we need to treat it with care. Do not touch or step on corals. We can also join groups working to protect reefs and the plants and animals that live there. These groups help to make people aware of how change and **pollution** can damage reefs.

Scientists believe most of the world's coral reefs could die out in the next 50 years unless we do something to prevent it.

Reef Know-how

A model is a **representation** of a real thing. Models can help us understand coral reefs better. They can show how different things are connected. Diagrams, storyboards, and drawings are all types of models.

Help others understand coral reefs better by creating your own model!

Create a Model

Make a storyboard model of a coral reef ecosystem. Your storyboard should have three different images. For example, you could show the Sun rising, fish and other animals using the reef for food, and animals seeking shelter on the reef.

Sun shines on coral reef

Plants grow, creating food for animals

Coral provides shelter for animals

Be sure to label each image on your storyboard.

A Deeper Understanding

Scientists use models to help them learn more about the ecosystem they are studying. Now it is your turn.

- Explain to your classmates how one of the living things in your storyboard is connected to other living and nonliving things in the ecosystem.
- How would the storyboard change if the living thing was gone from the ecosystem?

Learning more

Books

Gibbons, Gail. *Coral Reef.* Holiday House, 2010.

Priddy, Roger. *Smart Kids: Coral Reef.* Priddy Books, 2014.

Seymour, Simon. *Coral Reefs.* HarperCollins, 2013.

Websites

Kids Do Ecology: Coral Reef
http://kids.nceas.ucsb.edu/biomes/coralreef.html

Coral Reef Facts
www.coral-reef-info.com

World Wildlife Fund: Coral Reefs
http://wwf.panda.org/about_our_earth/blue_planet/coasts/coral_reefs/

Magic Porthole: Coral Reefs and Oceans
www.magicporthole.org

Defenders of Wildlife: Coral Reefs
www.defenders.org/coral-reef/basic-facts

Words to know

algae (AL-jee) noun Small plants without roots or stems that grow mainly in water

colony (KAH-luh-nee) noun A large group of animals that live together

ecosystem (EE-koh-sis-tuhm) noun All the living things in a place and their relation to the environment

energy (EN-ur-jee) noun The ability to do things

food chain (food chayn) noun An order of animals and plants in which each feeds on the one next in the chain

gills (GILLZ) noun The pair of organs near a fish's mouth through which it breathes

glands (glands) noun Area of the body that releases something

model (MOD-l) noun A representation of a real object

pollution [puh-LOO-shuh n] noun Harmful products in the environment

representation (rep-ri-zen-TEY-shuh n) noun A picture, drawing, model, or other copy of something

shelter (SHEL-tur) noun A place that offers protection

A noun is a person, place, or thing.

Index